INTRODUCTION

The Key lime, also known as the Mexican or West Indian lime, is a thin-skinned, small greenish-yellow juicy fruit known for its tart "one-of-a-kind" flavor. It's a most delicious fruit and has a great deal of versatility, but it's best known for the wonderful flavor it lends to pies and other desserts.

Key limes originated in Southeast Asia many centuries ago, and the story has often been told of how Columbus carried the seeds to Haiti in 1493 and planted some trees there. After the limes made their way to the Florida Keys they became a thriving commercial crop, only to be wiped out by the devastating hurricane of 1926. Since that time there have been several attempts to grow them commercially, but today most of the Key limes available are scattered throughout the Keys and are most often obtained from a tree in someone's backyard, or occasionally in the local markets.

If you are unable to obtain the real Key limes, you can easily substitute a Persian (or Tahiti or Bearss) lime that is readily available at any supermarket. For every three Key limes, you should substitute one Persian lime. Since many of these desserts are often made today with the Persian lime juice the flavor of your creation will still be excellent.

I've included some of my favorite recipes from Florida and the Florida Keys in this *Key Lime Desserts* book. The recipes are easy to prepare and even easier to enjoy. Bon Appetit!

FAMOUS *florida!* ®

KEY LIME DESSERTS

by Joyce LaFray

Seaside
Publishing, Inc.

Copyright 1996 **Joyce LaFray**

Published by **SeaSide Publishing, Inc.**

Send All Requests and Inquiries To:

$\mathcal{S}easide$
Publishing
P.O. Box 14441
St. Petersburg, FL 33733-4441
Phone: (813) 321 - 8840
Fax: (813) 321 - 8910

Manufactured in the United States of America
Member of the Publishers Association of the South

International Standard Book Number: 0-942084-65-9
Library of Congress Card Catalog Number: 87-063166

A **florida!**® Book

TABLE OF CONTENTS

PIES

COOKIES

FRUIT DESSERTS

CAKES

SOUFFLES

FROSTY DELIGHTS

PIES

DELICIOUS KEY LIME PIE
(ALLOW TIME TO CHILL)

1	tablespoon plain gelatin
1	cup sugar
¼	teaspoon salt
4	eggs, separated
½	cup Key lime or Persian lime juice, strained
¼	cup water
1	teaspoon grated Key lime or Persian lime peel
1	cup heavy cream, whipped
1	9-inch baked graham cracker crust, cooled (see page 19)

Mix the gelatin, half of the sugar, and salt in a sauce pan. In another pan, beat the egg yolks well. Add the Key lime juice and water to the egg yolk mixture. Stir the egg yolk mixture into the gelatin mixture. Cook over low heat, stirring constantly, just until the mixture comes to a boil. Remove from heat, stir in the grated peel. Chill, stirring occasionally, until the mixture mounds slightly when dropped from a spoon.

Beat the egg whites until soft peaks form. Gradually add the remaining sugar, beating until stiff. Fold into the chilled gelatin mixture. Fold in the whipped cream (some cream may be reserved for topping if desired). Pour into the baked graham cracker crust. Chill until firm.

Yield: **1 9-inch pie**

GREAT KEY LIME PIE
(ALLOW TIME TO CHILL)

FILLING:

1	cup sugar
¼	cup flour
3	tablespoons cornstarch
¼	teaspoon salt
2	cups water
3	egg yolks, beaten
1	tablespoon butter or margarine
¼	cup fresh Key lime or Persian lime juice, strained
1	teaspoon grated Key lime or Persian lime peel
1	9-inch baked graham cracker crust, cooled (see page 19)

MERINGUE:

4	egg whites
¼	teaspoon cream of tartar
6	teaspoons sugar

Combine the sugar, flour, cornstarch, and salt. Pour mixture in a large 2-quart saucepan and gradually stir in the water using a wire whisk. Cook over medium heat, stirring constantly, until thickened. Gradually stir the egg yolks into the hot mixture with a wire whisk. Return to heat and cook, stirring constantly, for 2 minutes. Whisk in the butter, Key lime juice, and Key lime peel. Cool slightly. Pour into the prepared graham cracker crust and chill.

Preheat the oven to 350°. To prepare the meringue, with an electric mixer, beat the egg whites and cream of tartar until foamy. Gradually beat in the sugar until stiff and glossy. Top the cooled pie with the meringue, spreading to seal edges and making peaks with the back of a small metal teaspoon by placing onto the egg white mixture and then lifting up to form peaks. Bake 5-6 minutes or until lightly golden.

Yield: 1 9-inch pie

FROZEN KEY LIME PIE
(ALLOW TIME TO CHILL)

½	cup Key lime or Persian lime juice, strained
1	cup sweetened condensed milk
6	egg whites*
2	tablespoons sugar
1	tablespoon grated Key lime or Persian lime peel
1	9-inch baked graham cracker crust, cooled (see page 19)
	Sweetened whipped cream for topping (optional)

Combine the Key lime juice and condensed milk, stirring until thick and smooth. Beat the egg whites until foamy and stiff. Add the sugar to the whites, 1 tablespoon at a time, and continue beating until stiff. Fold in the condensed milk mixture and blend well. Sprinkle the Key lime peel on the bottom of the pie shell. Turn the filling into the graham cracker crust. Chill until set. Freeze and keep until time to serve or serve without freezing. If topping is desired, swirl on sweetened whipped cream.

Yield: 1 9-inch pie

*Reserve the egg yolks for use in salads, casseroles, or other dishes.

KEY LIME ICE CREAM PIE

(ALLOW TIME TO CHILL)

½	cup and 3 tablespoons butter or margarine
½	cup sugar
1	egg, well beaten
3	tablespoons Key lime or Persian lime juice, strained
½	teaspoon grated Key lime or Persian lime peel
1 ¼	cup crushed vanilla wafers
⅓	cup finely chopped walnuts
1	quart vanilla ice cream, softened

Preheat the oven to 325°. To make the Key lime sauce, heat ¼ cup of butter and sugar until sugar dissolves. Add the egg. Cook until thick, stirring constantly. Add the Key lime juice, the 3 tablespoons of butter, and the grated Key lime peel. Remove from the stove and cool.

While this is cooling, mix the crushed vanilla wafers, walnuts, and ¼ cup of melted butter. Pat into a 9 x 9-inch pan. Bake for about 5-8 minutes or until the crust is slightly brown.

Spread the softened ice cream ¾-inch thick onto the crust and put it in the freezer until the ice cream is stiff. Add a layer of lime sauce. Pile more ice cream on, then another layer of lime sauce. Place back in freezer. Add another layer of ice cream—and continue for several layers. Refreeze.

Yield: 1 9 x 9-inch pie

INSTANT KEY LIME PIE
(ALLOW TIME TO CHILL)

1	6-ounce can frozen limeade, defrosted
1	14-ounce can sweetened condensed milk
1	24-ounce container Cool Whip
1	9-inch baked graham cracker crust, cooled (see page 19)
	Key lime or Persian lime slices for garnish

Place the frozen limeade, condensed milk, and Cool Whip in a bowl. Mix well. Pour into the prepared graham cracker crust. Refrigerate until set. Top with Key lime slices before serving.

Yield: 1 9-inch pie

KEY LIME SNOWBALL PIE

(ALLOW TIME TO CHILL)

1	envelope plain gelatin
¼	cup cold water
3	tablespoons sugar
1	cup light corn syrup
¼	cup Key lime or Persian lime juice, strained
1	teaspoon grated Key lime or Persian lime peel
½	teaspoon salt
5	egg whites*
1	9-inch baked graham cracker crust, cooled (see page 19)
	Key lime or Persian lime slices for garnish

Soften the gelatin in the cold water. Combine the sugar, half of the corn syrup, Key lime juice, grated peel, and salt in the top of a double boiler. Cook over hot water until slightly thickened.

Beat the egg whites until stiff. Gradually beat in the remaining corn syrup until the mixture is thick, full, and marshmallow-like. Fold the egg white mixture into the gelatin mixture and mix well. Pile the mixture lightly into the baked pie shell and freeze well until firm.

Garnish with half-slices of Key lime or Persian lime.

Yield: 1 9-inch pie

*Reserve the egg yolks for use in salad, casseroles, or other dishes.

MOUNTAIN-HIGH KEY LIME PIE
(ALLOW TIME TO CHILL)

4	**eggs, separated**
1	**can sweetened condensed milk**
½	**cup Key lime or Persian lime juice, strained**
1½	**teaspoons grated Key lime or Persian lime peel**
1	**9-inch baked graham cracker crust, cooled (see page 19)**
	Whipped topping or sweetened whipped cream for topping

Preheat the oven to 300°. Beat the yolks of 4 eggs and the white of 1 egg until thick and lemon-colored. Add the condensed milk and continue to beat well. Add the Key lime juice and grated Key lime peel. Beat until thick. Beat the 3 remaining egg whites until stiff and fold into the egg yolk mixture.

Pour into the pie shell and bake for 15 minutes. (Any extra filling can be baked in a glass custard cup along with the pie.)

Cool. Refrigerate for several hours before serving. Top "mountain-high" with whipped topping or sweetened whipped cream.

Yield: 1 9-inch pie

MRS. BIDDLE'S KEY LIME PIE
(ALLOW TIME TO CHILL)

1	14-ounce can sweetened condensed milk
4	egg yolks
½	cup Key lime or Persian lime juice, strained
1	9-inch baked graham cracker crust, cooled (see page 19)
	Freshly whipped cream

In an electric mixer, combine the milk and egg yolks at low speed. Slowly add the Key lime juice. Mix until well blended. Pour into the graham cracker crust and refrigerate overnight. Top with freshly whipped cream.

Yield: 1 9-inch pie

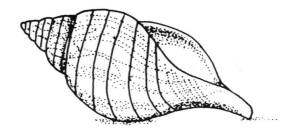

KEY LIME CHESS PIE

2	cups sugar
1	tablespoon flour
1	tablespoon corn meal
	Dash of salt
4	eggs
½	stick (¼ cup) butter or margarine, melted
¼	cup milk
¼	cup Key lime or Persian lime juice, strained
1	9-inch pastry shell, unbaked (see page 18)

Preheat the oven to 375°. Combine the sugar, flour, corn meal, and salt, tossing lightly. Add the eggs, butter, milk, and lime juice. Beat with an electric mixer at medium speed for 5 minutes. Pour into the pastry shell. Bake for 35-45 minutes or until the filling is set and top is golden brown. Cut while warm.

Yield: 1 9-inch pie

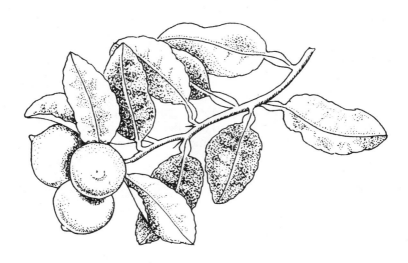

MARK'S MANGO KEY LIME PIE

CRUST:

½	pound graham cracker crumbs
1	tablespoon cake flour
2	tablespoons sugar
1	stick (½ cup) butter or margarine

FILLING:

¾	cup fresh Key lime or Persian lime juice, strained
1	medium ripe mango, peeled, seeded, and pureed
2¼	14-ounce cans sweetened condensed milk
6	egg yolks

MERINGUE:

4	egg whites
¾	cup sugar

Preheat the oven to 350°. Place the graham cracker crumbs, flour, sugar, and butter in a bowl and mix until blended. Pack into a 9-inch pie pan.

Mix the Key lime juice and mango puree. Add the condensed milk and egg yolks. Mix until blended. Pour into the crust. Bake for 7-10 minutes.

Place the egg whites and sugar in a stainless steel mixing bowl. Place the bowl over a pan of warm water and stir until the sugar is dissolved. The whites will become slightly warm. Remove the bowl from over the pan of water and beat the whites until stiff peaks form. Spread over the top of the pie and place under broiler until golden brown.

Yield: 1 9-inch pie

BLACK BOTTOM KEY LIME PIE

2	1-ounce squares semisweet chocolate
1	9-inch baked graham cracker crust, cooled (see page 19)
4	eggs, separated
¼	cup Key lime or Persian lime juice, strained
3	tablespoons water
1	teaspoon grated Key lime or Persian lime peel
1	cup sugar

In a double boiler, melt the chocolate over hot water. Spread the chocolate evenly over the pie shell. Beat the egg yolks in the top of a double boiler until thick and lemon-colored. Add the Key lime juice and water. Mix well. Stir in the Key lime peel and ½ cup of sugar. Cook over hot, but not boiling, water for about 12 minutes or until thick, stirring constantly. Remove from heat.

Beat the egg whites in a bowl until frothy. Gradually add the remaining sugar and beat until stiff peaks form. Fold half of the meringue into the egg yolk mixture and spread over the chocolate on the pie shell. Spoon the remaining meringue into a pastry tube and pipe onto the egg yolk mixture in a lattice design. Bake at 325° or 10-15 minutes or until meringue is lightly browned. Cool.

Yield: 1 9-inch pie

GOOD PIE PASTRY

1 ¼   **cups flour, sifted**
½   **teaspoon salt**
⅓   **cup margarine or lard, chilled**
¼   **cup ice water**

Place the flour and salt in a shallow mixing bowl. Cut in the shortening with a pastry blender until the mixture resembles coarse meal.

Sprinkle the water over the surface, a tablespoon at a time. Mix in lightly, with a fork, just until the pastry holds together. On a lightly floured surface, shape gently into a ball. Then, flatten into a circle about 1-inch thick, evening up the rough edges. Sprinkle lightly with flour.

Roll into a circle which is 12 inches in diameter using a rolling pin and short, firm strokes. Transfer the pastry to a 9-inch pie pan by laying the rolling pin across the center of the pastry circle. Fold half of the pastry over the rolling pin and ease into the pan. Press slightly. Seal any cracks or holes by pressing dampened scraps of pastry on top. Trim pastry so it hangs evenly one inch over the rim of the pan. Roll the overhang under, even with the rim and crimp or flute as desired.

To bake an unfilled pastry pie crust, preheat the oven to 425° Prick the bottom and sides of the pastry with a fork. Lay a large square of wax paper over the crust and fill with uncooked rice or dried beans. Bake for 10-12 minutes or until just brown. Carefully lift out the wax paper full of rice or beans. Cool before filling.

Yield: **1 9-inch pie crust**

GRAHAM CRACKER CRUST

1 ¼   **cups graham cracker crumbs**
¼   **cup sugar**
½   **stick (¼ cup) butter or margarine**

Preheat the oven to 325°. Mix the graham cracker crumbs and sugar together. Melt the butter and mix well with the crumbs. Press into a 9-inch pie pan. Bake for 8 minutes.

Yield: 1 9-inch pie crust

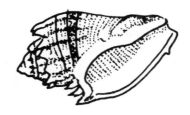

COOKIES

KEY LIME DROP COOKIES

1	stick (½ cup) butter or margarine, softened
1	cup sugar
2	teaspoons grated Key lime or Persian lime peel
1	egg, lightly beaten
½	cup Key lime or Persian lime juice, strained
3	cups flour
½	teaspoon cinnamon
4	teaspoons baking powder

Preheat the oven to 375°. In a mixing bowl, cream together the butter, sugar, and Key lime peel. Beat in the egg and Key lime juice. In another bowl, sift the flour, cinnamon, and baking powder together and beat into the butter mixture.

Drop by teaspoonfuls onto an ungreased baking sheet. Bake for 10 minutes or until very light brown. Remove immediately to cooling rack. Cookies will be cake-like.

Yield: 4-5 dozen

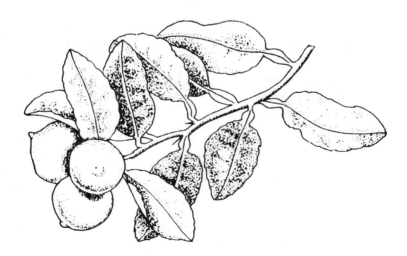

The Blueberry Patch, Brooksville, Florida

KEY LIME DELIGHTS

2	cups flour
½	cup powdered sugar
2	sticks (1 cup) butter or margarine
4	eggs
2	cups sugar
	Dash of salt
⅓	cup Key lime or Persian lime juice, strained
	Powdered sugar

Preheat the oven to 350°. In a bowl, combine the flour and powdered sugar. Cut in the butter. Press the mixture into a 13 x 9-inch baking pan. Bake for 20-25 minutes or until golden brown.

Meanwhile, beat the eggs at high speed with an electric mixer until light and pale yellow in color. Gradually add the sugar and salt. Then, add the Key lime juice, continuing to beat at high speed. Pour over the hot crust and return to the oven for 20-25 minutes longer or until golden brown.

Remove from the oven and sprinkle at once with powdered sugar. Cool. Cut into squares.

Makes: About 4-dozen bars

Wakulla Springs Lodge, Wakulla Springs, Florida

KEY LIME COOKIES

½	cup butter or margarine
1 ½	cups unsifted powdered sugar
1	egg
1	tablespoon Key lime or Persian Lime juice
2	teaspoons grated Key lime or Persian lime peel
1	cup all-purpose flour
	teaspoon baking powder
¼	teaspoon salt
2	cups Kelloggs cornflakes, crushed

Preheat over 350°. Beat together the butter and sugar until smooth. Add the egg, Key lime juice, and peel. Mixture may appear curdled. Stir in the flour, baking powder, and salt.

Place the crushed cornflakes in a bowl and drop cookie batter by teaspoonfuls into cornflakes and toss to coat. Place the cookies on an ungreased cookie sheet. Bake for 16 minutes. Cool on a rack.

Yield: **About 2 dozen**

FRUIT
DESSERTS

LUSCIOUS FRUIT DESSERT

(ALLOW TIME TO MARINATE OVERNIGHT)

⅓	cup Key lime or Persian lime juice, strained
⅓	cup honey
½	cup light dry sherry
1	quart cut up assorted fresh fruits: strawberries, peaches, plums, bananas, pineapple, papaya, grapes
	Salad greens
	Freshly shaved coconut for garnish

In a small bowl, blend well the Key lime juice, honey, and sherry. Let stand until the honey dissolves. Pour the marinade over the fruit. Let stand for a minimum of 2 hours or overnight, tossing occasionally. Drain. Arrange the fruit in small glass bowls lined with greens. Garnish with coconut.

Serves: 6-8

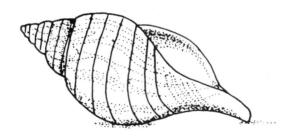

FLORIDA FRUIT BOWL
(ALLOW TIME TO CHILL)

2	cups water
1½	cups sugar
3	tablespoons Key lime or Persian lime juice, strained
2	tablespoons anise seeds
½	teaspoon salt
1	small pineapple, peeled, cored, and cut into 1-inch chunks
1	small honeydew melon, peeled and cut into 1-inch chunks
1	small cantaloupe, peeled and cut into 1-inch chunks
2	oranges, peeled and sectioned
2	large nectarines, sliced into wedges
½	pound seedless green grapes, sliced in half
2	kiwifruit, peeled and sliced

In a 2-quart saucepan, cook the water, sugar, Key lime juice, anise seeds, and salt over medium heat for 15 minutes or until the mixture becomes a light syrup. Refrigerate until the syrup is cool.

In a large bowl, combine the pineapple, honeydew melon, cantaloupe, oranges, nectarines, and grapes. Pour the chilled syrup through a strainer over the fruit. Cover and refrigerate until well chilled, stirring occasionally.

Just before serving, gently stir the kiwifruit slices into the fruit mixture.

Serves: 12

JAMAICAN-STYLE KEY LIME BANANAS

1	stick (½ cup) butter or margarine
1	cup sugar
¼	cup water
¼	cup Tia Maria liqueur
1	tablespoon Key lime or Persian lime juice, strained
1	teaspoon vanilla extract
	Grated peel of 3 Key limes or 1 Persian lime
8	small bananas
1	quart vanilla ice cream

In a saucepan, melt the butter. Add the sugar and water. Cook on a low boil until reduced to a heavy syrup (about 15-20 minutes). Add the Tia Maria, Key lime juice, vanilla, and Key lime peel.

Peel and slice the bananas in half lengthwise, then in half crosswise. Add the bananas to the hot syrup and cover until just warm. (The syrup may be prepared ahead and reheated along with the bananas just before serving.) Serve warm, not hot, in stemmed dessert dishes over vanilla ice cream.

Serves: 6-8

CAKES

KEY LIME CAKE SUPREME

1	cup evaporated milk
²/₃	cup sugar
	Juice of 3 Key limes or 1 Persian lime, strained
½	teaspoon vanilla extract
	Grated Key lime or Persian lime peel
1	9-inch sponge cake or rum cake

Chill the milk. Beat with an electric mixer until foamy. Add the sugar. Whip again. Add the Key lime juice, Key lime peel, and vanilla extract. Blend well. Serve over sponge cake or rum cake.

Serves: 6-8

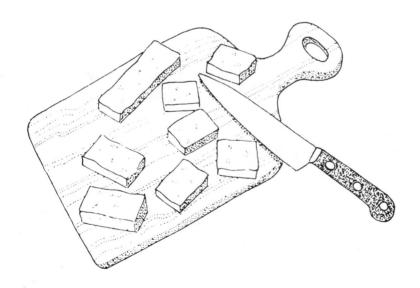

Lime Tree Bay Cafe, Long Key, Florida

EASY FLORIDA KEY LIME CHEESECAKE

(ALLOW TIME TO CHILL)

FILLING:

1	cup heavy cream
2	envelopes unflavored gelatin
1 ¾	cups sugar
	Dash of salt
1	cup milk
2	eggs, well beaten
1	24-ounce carton (3 cups) creamed cottage cheese
¼	cup Key lime or Persian lime juice, strained

CRUMB TOPPING:

¾	cup graham cracker crumbs
1	tablespoon sugar
2	tablespoons butter or margarine, softened

Whip the heavy cream and chill. Mix the gelatin, sugar, and salt togetther in the top of a double boiler. Stir in the milk and beaten eggs. Cook over boiling water, stirring constantly, for about 5 minutes or until the gelatin is dissolved.

Blend the cottage cheese and lime juice with an electric mixer or in the blender on high speed until smooth. Add the gelatin mixture and mix well. Stir in whipped cream and blend well to avoid lumps. Pour into an 8 x 8 x 2-inch-square pan or pyrex dish. Chill until partially set.

Combine topping ingredients and sprinkle over filling. Chill until firm.

Serves: 10-12

Whitey's Fish Camp, Orange Park, Florida.

MANGO CAKE WITH KEY LIME FROSTING

CAKE:

½	cup margarine or butter
1 ½	cups sugar
3	eggs
½	cup vegetable oil
2	cups sifted flour
2	teaspoons baking soda
½	teaspoon salt
2	teaspoons cinnamon
½	cup raisins
¼	cup coconut flakes
2	cups peeled and chopped ripe mangoes
1	teaspoon vanilla

KEY LIME FROSTING:

	Juice of 3 Key limes or 1 Persian lime, strained
1	cup confectioner's sugar

Preheat the oven to 350°. Grease well two loaf pans. Cream the margarine and sugar until light and fluffy. Beat in the eggs. Add the oil. Set the batter aside.

Mix the flour, baking soda, salt, and cinnamon together. Dredge the raisins and coconut in a little flour. Add the remainder of the flour mixture to the batter. Fold in the raisins, coconut, and mangoes. Add the vanilla. Let stand for about 20 minutes.

Divide the batter into the two loaf pans and place in the oven.

The bread will be done when a wire tester or toothpick comes out clean.

Mix Key lime juice with confectioner's sugar, blend well, and frost while cake is hot. Add more juice, if necessary.

Yield: 2 loaves

SOUFFLES

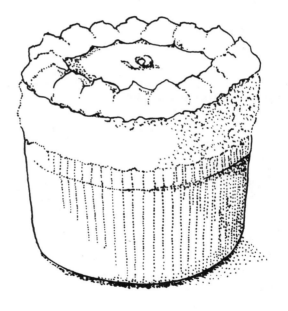

KEY LIME SOUFFLE

1   cup heavy cream
1   envelope unflavored gelatin
¼   cup cold water
1   cup sugar
4   eggs, separated plus 2 egg whites
½   cup Key lime or Persian lime juice, strained
½   teaspoon salt
1   tablespoon grated Key lime or Persian lime peel
     Fresh coconut shavings, lightly toasted
     Sliced maraschino cherries for garnish

Whip the heavy cream until stiff and chill. Sprinkle the gelatin over the water to soften. In the top of a double boiler, mix ½ cup of sugar, egg yolks, Key lime juice, and salt. Cook in a double boiler, stirring constantly, until slightly thickened. Remove from heat. Stir in the softened gelatin and Key lime peel. Stir the mixture until gelatin is completely dissolved. Cool.

Beat the egg whites until stiff. Beat in ½ cup of sugar gradually until whites hold definite peaks. Fold the whipped cream and egg white mixture into the Key lime mixture. Spoon into souffle dish. Chill.

Before serving, sprinkle with fresh coconut flakes and decorate with sliced maraschino cherries.

Serves: **4-6**

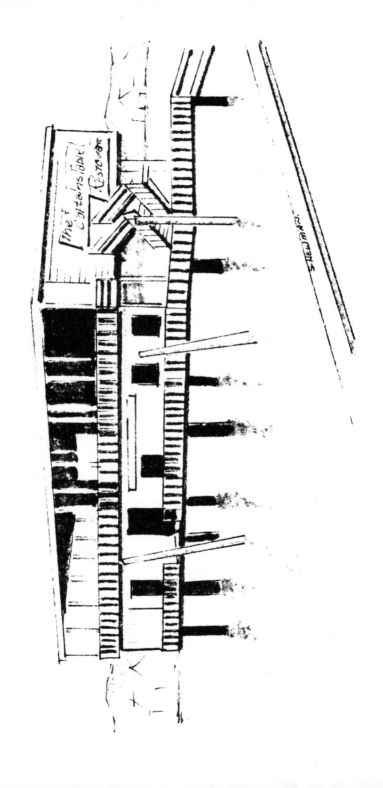

The Lighteansdale
Restaurant

S. NEWMAN.

FROZEN KEY LIME SOUFFLE

5	large eggs, separated
¾	cup sugar, divided
1	cup coconut rum
3	tablespoons Key lime or Persian lime juice, strained
1	teaspoon grated Key lime or Persian lime peel
1	cup heavy cream, whipped
½	cup finely chopped nuts
	Whipped cream and lime slices for garnish

Cut wax paper or aluminum foil into eight strips which are 2-inches wide and long enough to go around eight 5-ounce individual souffle dishes. Fasten the strips to the souffle dishes securely with string or tape to form a collar to hold the souffle mixture above the dish until it sets.

In a small bowl, beat the egg yolks with ¼ cup of sugar for the remaining ½ cup of sugar, beating until the whites are stiff and Key lime juice, and Key lime peel.

In a large bowl, beat the egg whites until foamy. Gradually add the remaining 1/2 cup of sugar, beating until the whites are stiff and glossy. Fold the egg yolks into the beaten egg whites. Fold in the whipped cream.

Spoon into prepared souffle dishes. Freeze overnight. To serve, remove collar and press the chopped nuts around the edge of the souffle. Garnish with additional whipped cream and lime slices.

Serves: 8

FROSTY
DELIGHTS

KEY LIME RUM SHERBET
(ALLOW TIME TO CHILL)

2	cups sugar
2	cups water
4	teaspoons gelatin soaked in ½ cup cold water
⅔	cup Key lime or Persian lime juice, strained
1	cup white rum
¼	teaspoon salt
4	egg whites

Boil the sugar and water for 10 minutes. Add softened gelatin and when it has dissolved, remove from the heat. Add the Key lime juice and rum. Freeze for 1 hour in 2 ice trays. Remove to a chilled bowl and beat with an electric mixer until frothy. Add the salt to the egg whites. Beat stiff and fold into the other mixture. Return to ice trays and freeze until firm.

Serves: 8-10

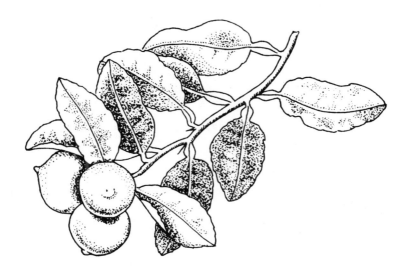

A TASTE OF HEAVEN

(ALLOW TIME TO CHILL

1   **cup heavy whipping cream**
¼   **cup sugar**
            Grated peel of 3 Key limes or 1 Persian lime
            Juice of 3 Key limes or 1 Persian lime, strained
⅓   **cup light rum**
            Sliced maraschino cherries for garnish

      With an electric mixer, whip the cream, starting at low speed and working up to high speed. When the cream forms peaks, whip in the sugar. Bring the mixer to low speed. Then, add the peel to the cream. Gradually add the juice. Beat well and add the rum. Pour into 6 small dessert cups. Chill thoroughly for about 1 hour. Garnish with sliced maraschino cherries.

Serves: **6**

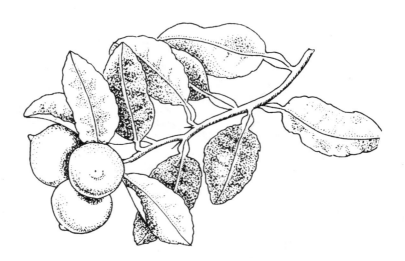

KEY LIME ORANGE ICE
(ALLOW TIME TO CHILL)

2	**cups orange juice**
2	**cups sugar**
1	**cup Key lime or Persian lime juice, strained**
	Mint leaves for garnish

Mix thoroughly and pour into a freezing tray for about 1 hour. To serve, garnish each serving with mint leaves.

Serves: 2-4

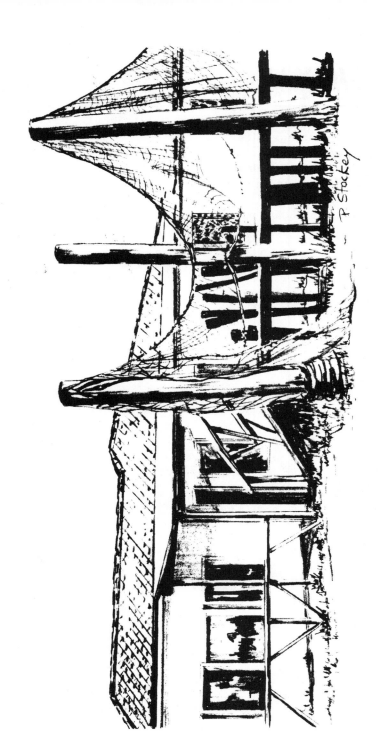

The Vilano Seafood Shack, Vilano Beach, Florida

~ P. Stockey

KEY LIME TROPICAL ICE
(ALLOW TIME TO CHILL)

	Juice of 2 medium-sized oranges, strained
	Juice of 9 Key limes or 3 Persian limes, strained
2	bananas, mashed
¼	cup sugar
¼	cup water
	Mint leaves for garnish

Mix thoroughly all the ingredients and place in freezing tray for about 1 hour.

Garnish each serving with fresh mint leaves.

Serves:　　**2**

SPANISH CREAM WITH KEY LIME TOPPING

(ALLOW TIME TO CHILL)

2	cups milk
1	tablespoon gelatin
3	eggs, separated
1	cup sugar
1	teaspoon vanilla
1	cup sliced fresh strawberries
1	cup whipped cream
1	teaspoon grated Key lime or Persian lime peel

Chill and grease a standard ring mold. Heat the milk and gelatin in a double boiler. In a separate bowl beat the egg yolks and add sugar. Add this egg yolk mixture to the milk mixture and stir while the custard thickens. Remove from stove.

Beat the egg whites and add the vanilla. Slowly add the custard to the egg white mixture. Pour into a greased and chilled ring mold. Chill for several hours. When ready to serve, top with fresh strawberries and whipped cream to which a teaspoon of grated Key lime peel has been added.

Serves: 6-8

FAMOUS FLORIDA! ®

FAMOUS FLORIDA!® SERIES

SeaSide Publishing offers a luscious harvest in the slim volumes that make up our **Famous Florida!** cookbook series. Each offers a generous serving of the state's unique bounty and heritage: crab, conch, seafood, Key lime, orange and Seminole Indian recipes.

This series is a repository of specialties from some of the best restaurants in the state. Many of the creations are found nowhere else.